O N E

The seasons are passing at a ferocious pace!

—ONE

Manga creator ONE began *One-Punch Man* as a webcomic, which quickly went viral, garnering over 10 million hits. In addition to *One-Punch Man*, ONE writes and draws the series *Mob Psycho 100* and *Makai no Ossan*.

Y U S U K E M U R A T A

I believe I can solve 90 percent of my problems through sheer force of will.

—Yusuke Murata

A highly decorated and skilled artist best known for his work on *Eyeshield 21*, Yusuke Murata won the 122nd Hop Step Award (1995) for *Partner* and placed second in the 51st Akatsuka Award (1998) for *Samui Hanashi*.

ONE-PUNCH MAN | 28

ONE + YUSUKE MURATA

☆THE STORIES, CHARACTERS, AND INCIDENTS

MENTIONED IN THIS PUBLICATION
ARE ENTIRELY FICTIONAL.

SAITAMA

FLASHY FLASH

TANK-TOP MASTER

ATOMIC SAMURAI

MUMEN RIDER

OCULETTE

CHILD EMPEROR

GENOS

CHARACTERS

CONTENTS

ONE-PUNCH MAN VOL.28

STORY

Gyoro-Gyoro, the supposed brains of the Monster Association, is revealed to be a decoy for the psychic Psychos, the true mastermind. Finding herself on the losing end of a fierce battle against Tornado, Psychos fuses with the Monster King Orochi and accesses unbelievable power. A frightful battle between psychics ensues. Seeing an opening, Psychos delivers a grievous wound to Tornado.

However, Genos arrives to assist Tornado, thereby earning Psychos's wrath. Meanwhile, Saitama is digging out Flashy Flash from a mound of rubble in the underground labyrinth …

PUNCH 138: **THE WRINGER**

WHSH

GASHAN

GR-AA-AA-AA-AH!

HA! YOU CAN'T OVER-POWER ME HEAD-ON!

TORNADO!

P-TOOM

DO IT NOW!!

!!

YOU SPLIT UP MY BLAST!

SPROO

OOSH

YANK

KTUNK

BTONK

KRUNK

RISE AND SHINE!

GASP!

GRNK

GYAH!
GWUNK

TOONK

GOT 'EM!

KYAH!
GRASH

GUH!

!!

SHWAAAA AA

FINALLY, I CAN FOCUS ON THIS FIGHT!

HEH...

I DID NOT DO IT FOR YOU.

WELL DONE, DEMON CYBORG.

HWOOM

YOU SAID SOME-THING EAR-LIER.

...A SINGLE FINGER!!

NGH!

GR

N CH

I CAN'T MOVE...

YOUR NAME...

HWISH

...IS PSYCHOS, RIGHT?

YOU THREAT-ENED MY SISTER.

MY SISTER'S CONCENTRATION HAS IMPROVED!

IS HER PSYCHIC ABILITY LIMITLESS?

THE POWER UP THERE IS INCREASING!

....!

WHOA...

YOU'RE A MON-STER!

HWM

Y-YOU STILL HAD MORE TO GIVE?!

SHE INTENDS TO FINISH THIS!

R M

M

HMM?

NO
...

...

A TECHNICAL GLITCH?

OPERATOR, THE MAP OF CITY Z IS WARPING.

THE *CITY* IS BEING TWISTED.

THEY'RE BLEEDING!

...SO YOU GOTTA **WRING** IT OUT!

AN OLD RAG CAN ABSORB A LOT...

DRILL!

KA-MA!

WHAT IS THIS? BLOOD?!

PTOO! PTOO!

SPURT

WHOA!

IAI!

Z Z T   Z Z T   Z Z T

ZOMBIE-MAN! RESPOND!

RMM

WHERE'S ZOMBIE-MAN?!

ZOMBIE-MAN!

PLOP

THE R-ROCK IS SHIFTING!

KRNNNCH

GAH!

RMM

WHAT'M I SUPPOSED TO DO?!

HEY! DID YOUR BOSS DO THIS?! KNOCK IT OFF! IT'LL WRECK MY HOUSE!

NO, BE CAREFUL!

TOSS TOSS TOSS TOSS

I'LL GET YOU OUT IN A JIFFY!

THEN WE CAN'T AFFORD TO BE CAREFUL!

YIKES!

RMMMM

WHEEZ WHEEZ

RMB

RMB RMB

MORE CLIMBING?!

PUNCH 139: GIANT BARRIER

...?!

!

TORNADO?

BLRFT

...

OUR BARRIER FADED.

HM?

FWSH

IS MY SISTER ALL RIGHT?!

A DISRUPTION TO HER PSYCHIC WAVES?!

DID I USE TOO MUCH POWER AT ONCE?

PANG

KOFF

PANG

WHAT?! WHY NOW?!

THIS IS OUR CHANCE!

SHE SUDDENLY LET UP!

SMOKE SCREEN!

PWOOM

?!

KRAK

PWOP

SNAP

I'LL SUCK BLOOD FROM THE CITY'S INHABITANTS!

THIS SMOKE IS GOOEY!

GWOoooo

EW...

...?!

I SENSE HER IN MANY DIRECTIONS!!

HA HA HA! I LEARNED A NEW TRICK!

FORTUNE IS ON MY SIDE!

EVEN TERRIBLE TORNADO HAS LIMITS!

HUH ?!

KRUM

BLE

SMASH

BASH

BOOM

VROOOSH

AAGH!

UH-OH
...

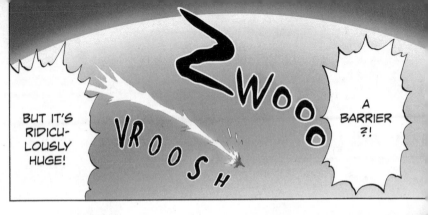

BUT IT'S RIDICULOUSLY HUGE!

ZWOOO

VROOSH

A BARRIER?!

● REINFORCED DOUBLE BARRIER

● CONVENTIONAL BARRIER

...SO YOU CAN'T GET OUT!

↑ ↑ ↑ ↑

REPULSION

REPULSION

POWER PASSES OUT

I'VE TAKEN PRECAUTIONS AGAINST BARRIER REVERSAL...

EVEN REVERSED, NOTHING GETS OUT

REVERSED

※SHE ALSO USED THIS TYPE WHEN RESCUING THE HEROES.

SIMPLY MAINTAINING THAT BARRIER WILL KEEP YOU BUSY!

HEH!

GA WP

...I'LL SPEAR YOU THROUGH THE HEART!

PWOOM

SHOOM

PSS

ULP
...

BSHOOM

FOUND
YOU!

THERE'S ANOTHER AIRCRAFT!

THAT CREEP'S ALIVE?!

IS THAT DRIVE KNIGHT?

GWOOOSH

GWAWWW

LOWER ORGANISMS CANNOT STAND AGAINST...

ANOTHER HERO?!

...THE APEX OF EVOLU-TION!

VREEE

THE ESSENCE OF EVOLU-TION IS CONFLICT!

YOU'RE HERE TOO?!

PSHHH

DEMON CY-BORG!

KRAK

KRAK

KRAK

SLAM

OH MY!

I MUST GO HELP.

RIGHT NOW TERRIBLE TORNADO IS STOPPING THE MONSTER ASSOCIA-TION'S BOSS WITH A GIANT BARRIER. SHE IS AT HER LIMIT, BUT DRIVE KNIGHT HAS ALSO JOINED THE FIGHT.

I WILL EXPLAIN IN DETAIL LATER...

AND I ASK FOR YOUR SUPPORT.

BLECH...

TCH... NO TIME FOR STANDING AROUND. IT'S OUT OF RANGE, BUT I'LL TRY MY FLYING SWORD!

HUH?

WHSH

TH

WSSH

GLORP GLORP

BLORFF

YUCK!

PIG GOD!

YOU PROTECTED EVERYONE INSIDE YOUR STOMACH?!

SPLOOOOOSH

WHAT THE?!

POK POK

NO, I'M JUST WOUNDED...

IT LOOKS LIKE YOU DIGESTED ZOMBIE-MAN!!

GAAAAAH!!

W-WHERE AM I?

GASP!

PIG GOD...

THE OTHER SWORDSMEN ARE ALL RIGHT TOO.

IT WAS EASY BECAUSE YOU GATHERED EVERYONE IN ONE PLACE.

KLANK

PHEW...

Aw, it was nothing.

HOW CAN I THANK YOU?!

I AM DEEPLY GRATEFUL!

OH...

...I SEE...

I'M STILL A LONG WAY FROM CLASS S...

I NEED ANOTHER WAY.

I CAN'T REACH.

CLUMP

IAI!

!

M...

MASTER!

SOMEHOW...
I SURVIVED!

WELL
DONE!

...

CLASP

WE COULDN'T EVEN BUDGE THAT RUBBLE...

ANY-ONE ELSE IN NEED OF RESCUE?!

HOW DO YOU DO THAT?

WHOA!

UMPH!

IT'S TANK-TOP MAGIC!

HUH?

MAG-IC.

YES, THANKS TO A LIFT FROM YOU.

MASTER, I'M GLAD YOU CAME.

?

HM?

HEEEY! OVER HERE!

WE'VE GOT WOUNDED!

LOOK!

THE RESCUE HELI-COPTER!

THE SITUATION HAS REACHED **EXTREME PROPORTIONS.**

IT'S MASSIVE!

THRUM THRUM

A BARRIER... IS TORNADO HERE?

...

STAY HERE AND CONTINUE THE RESCUE OP!

I NEED TO GIVE HER BACK-UP!

MUMEN RIDER!

TUMP

HUH?

UH, YEAH.

LIGHTNING MAX, IS TORNADO AT THAT TOWER?

KRUNK

GWUP

I'M GONNA MAKE IT SO YOU CAN CARRY OUT THE WOUNDED SOON!

BE CAREFUL.

UNDER-STOOD.

YOU TOO!

Hwooo

.....!!

MAYBE I SHOULD WEAR ONE TOO...

DOES HIS TANK-TOP HAVE ANYTHING TO DO WITH THAT...?

VREEE BABOOSH

FWOOSH!

ALL RIGHT, BACK TO RESCUING PEOPLE!

COOPER-ATION, HUH?

Five minutes ago...

...AND NOW TERRIBLE TORNADO IS BATTLING THE MONSTER ASSOCIATION'S LEADER!

A TOWER SPLIT THE EARTH'S CRUST AND ROSE OVERHEAD...

I'D LIKE TO TAKE SAMPLES OF THE FLESH LYING AROUND, BUT I'M LOW ON ENERGY.

SO I'LL HELP MYSELF!

THIS IS JUST WHAT I NEED.

I'M STILL NO MATCH FOR UGLINESS!!

IN THE END, ALL I COULD DO WAS COVER MY EYES AND COWER LIKE A BABY!

...BUT NOW LOOK AT ME!

I TALKED BIG BEFORE JOINING THIS FIGHT...

HUH
?!

DID THEY OVERHEAR ME PANICKING TO TORNADO OVER MY TRANSMITTER?!

GASP

WHY ARE THEY STARING AT ME?

URGH...

HOW DARE THEY LOOK AT ME—A TRUE HERO—WITH ANYTHING BUT ENVY!

THOSE SCUMBAGS!

YOU DON'T LOOK WELL, SO MAYBE YOU SHOULD JOIN THE REAR GUARD.

UH... HI, AMAI.

THE BRAT! HE'S ONLY ADDING TO MY SHAME!!

IS HE TREATING ME WITH PITY?!

I BET SEKINGAR OVERHEARD TOO...

ME? IN THE REAR GUARD?

I OF ALL PEOPLE DO NOT DESERVE THIS!!

OH, THE DIS- GRACE !!

THANKS.

BUT I ACCEPT YOUR PROPOS- AL.

ONLY A CHILD WOULD SPEAK SO FOOL- ISHLY!

...IT WILL RUIN THE SUPERSTAR STATUS I HAVE WORKED SO HARD TO ATTAIN.

IF WORD OF THIS REACHES HERO ASSOCIATION HEADQUARTERS...

I MUST COVER UP MY FAILURE.

...DUE TO A COWARDLY MONSTER'S ATTACK FROM THE REAR!

NO ONE WOULD FIND IT SUSPICIOUS IF EVERYONE HERE WERE TO DIE...

MWA HA HA ...

...YOU DON'T LOOK SO WELL.

HEY...

KLAN

ARE YOU ALL RIGHT?

NNNGH...

URNGH!

WHAT'S WRONG ?!

HEY, STOP THAT!

BAM

BAM

ARRRRGH!

I CAN HANDLE THIS.

SPARE ME YOUR CON-CERN.

HUFF!

HUFF!

HUFF!

...OF BEING COOL.

I ALMOST FORGOT THE FOUNDA-TION...

THAT'S WHY YOU'RE SO UPSET?

I JUST NOTICED MY OUTFIT ISN'T WELL COORDINATED.

PUNCH 141:
UNCONQUERABLE

GARO DEFEATED YOU?!

HOW CAN ANYONE EVEN BEAT THIS GUY?

YOU DIDN'T WIN? IN HAND-TO-HAND COMBAT?!

THERE MAY BE NO ONE WHO CAN STOP HIM.

...SO HE'LL REAPPEAR SOON.

GARO IS ALIVE...

I DON'T UNDERSTAND IT!

...STRONGER AND FIERCER THAN EVER!

N-NO MATTER WHAT YOU DO, HE GETS BACK UP...

...THE KIND OF EVIL I WANT TO COMMIT.

YES... I JUST REALIZED...

MAYBE IT'S JUST DUE TO THAT HUMAN MEATBALL'S PUNCHES, BUT MY HEAD FEELS CLEARER!

BUT WHAT'S HAPPENING TO ME? THE MORE I GET BEATEN DOWN, THE STRONGER I GET!

...THAT I CAN REACH THREAT LEVEL GOD!

NOW I'M CONFIDENT...

...I'LL CAST THE HUMAN RACE INTO AN ABYSS OF FEAR!

AND THEN...

EVERYONE
EVERYWHERE
WILL CRINGE
IN FEAR...

...IN
THANKFULNESS
AT SIMPLY
BEING ALIVE.

...AND
JOIN
HANDS...

BULLYING AND
DISCRIMINATION...

...AND
EVEN
WAR.

IN A WORLD
WHERE MERE
SURVIVAL IS
A STRUGGLE,
EVIL DEEDS
WILL VANISH.

INJUSTICE
AND THOSE
RESPONSIBLE
FOR IT WILL
DISAPPEAR.

THE SNOTTY BRAT?!

H-HOW WERE YOU ABLE TO FIND ME?

OLD DUDE!

I DON'T ACTUALLY CARE ABOUT JUSTICE OR—

I UNDER-STAND YOUR ANGER.

AMAI MASK ...

WHOK

WHOK

WHOK

WHOK

HEY!

WE DON'T NEED COWARDS HERE, SO GET LOST!

ARE YOU A HERO OR NOT ?!

SELF-PITY! WHINING! AND EXCUSES!

I'M TRULY SORRY.

BUT WEREN'T YOU ALSO FALLING APART EARLIER?

...YOU...

SUPER-ALLOY BLACK-LUSTER...

HEY, YOU HAVE NO RIGHT TO—

YOU'RE STILL A HUNK OF MUSCLE! AND SUPER-STRONG!

B-BUT EVEN THOSE KICKS FROM AMAI DIDN'T HURT YOU!

WE WILL DEFINITELY NEED YOUR STRENGTH...

GARO AND THE LEADERS OF THE MONSTER ASSOCIATION ARE STILL ALIVE.

...TO BEAT THEM!

I'M
THE
SAME
WAY.

I'VE
ENCOUN-
TERED
DIFFICULTIES
...

...
AND I'VE DISAP-POINTED MYSELF...

...BUT I GET BACK UP AND KEEP MOVING FORWARD.

THAT'S
WHAT
HEROES
DO.

WHAT DOES YOUR **PRIDE** SAY?

SO TELL ME!

TRMBL TRMBL

N N N G H ...

GET UP OR I'LL DEEP KISS YOU.

N N N G H ...

...

IN THAT CASE...

...WE SHOULD COOPERATE IN TAKING THAT THING DOWN!!

...

YOU WANT TO COOPERATE?!

HUH ?!

SHALL I STRIKE YOU ALL DOWN?

CAREFUL WHAT YOU EAT.

HAVE YOU EATEN SOMETHING WEIRD?

YOU'D PUT YOUR BUTT IN OUR HANDS?!

YOU? THE HIGH-AND-MIGHTY WARRIOR?

JUST THIS ONCE! AND ONLY BECAUSE I RECOGNIZE THEIR STRENGTH!

HMPH!

What changed?

MASTER !!

HM?

WHAT DO YOU HAVE IN MIND?

POT POT

SPINNN

IS TERRIBLE TORNADO UP THERE?

HWOMP

I CAME TO LEND SUPPORT!

TANK-TOP MASTER!

WHAT'S THE SITUATION?

GLOMP

HM?

WELCOME BACK!!

I THINK IT'S GONNA WORK OUT.

AMAI MASK
...

...BUT I'VE CHANGED MY MIND.

I THOUGHT YOU WERE ALL TALK...

HA HA HA!

YOU REALLY **ARE** CREEPY...

WHY NOW?

...

I NEVER THOUGHT THEY WOULD COOPERATE.

THEY RAN INTO A WALL, BUT GREW AND FOUND A NEW WAY FORWARD!

THEY REALLY **ARE** CLASS-S HEROES!

NO, DON'T FIGHT!

DON'T WORRY, AWRY MASK.

...BUT DON'T HOLD ME BACK.

I DON'T EXPECT MUCH FROM A GUY THE ENEMY **DENUDED** ...

PUNCH 142:
RESONANCE

HELLO.

TUMP

MIND IF **WE** JOIN?

WHAT A COINCI- DENCE.

WHAT ?!

GOOD QUESTION. AFTER ALL, YOU **EXCLUDED** ME FROM THE MISSION.

W- WHAT ARE YOU DOING HERE ?!

BANG ?!

BANG!

YEAH, W-WELL...

...I HAD A REASON FOR THAT.

YOU SAID HE WASN'T PARTICIPATING BECAUSE YOU COULDN'T REACH HIM.

WHAT DOES HE MEAN, CHILD EMPEROR?

HEH... GIVEN MY RECORD, PERHAPS THAT'S UNDERSTAND-ABLE.

YOU WERE WORRIED THAT I'D GO SOFT ON GARO BECAUSE HE'S A FORMER PUPIL.

I WILL TAKE RESPON-SIBILITY BY DEFEATING HIM WITH MY OWN FISTS.

BUT DO NOT WORRY.

SO REMOVING ME FROM THE MISSION WAS FOR THE BEST. I OWE YOU ONE, BOY.

ACTUALLY, I **PREFER** SETTLING THIS AS HIS FORMER MASTER TO DOING SO AS A HERO.

I'LL HELP IN ANY WAY I CAN!

PLEASE! WE MUST HURRY IF WE'RE TO HELP MY SISTER!!

HELLISH BLIZZARD ...

...

I SUSPECT MY SISTER IS ALREADY UNCON-SCIOUS!!

AAAUGH!

TORNADOOO!!

I MUST DEFEAT HER!

FWWSH

BWOOM

TCH!

SHE'S UNCON-SCIOUS.

TORNA-DO...

WHO...?

...THAT SOMEONE WILL COME HELP.

YOU SHOULDN'T INTERFERE.

DON'T GIVE ME HOPE...

...at a certain research facility.

Eighteen years ago...

GRARRRRRR

RUUUN!

GYAAAH! A SYNTHETIC BEAST BROKE FREE!!

VREEE VREEE

LET ME OUT OF HERE!

DON'T LEAVE ME!

WAIT!

101

ALL PERSONNEL, EVACUATE!

TROMP TROMP

PRIORITIZE SAVING SUBJECTS WITH GREATER PROMISE!

NO! HER NUMBERS HAVE LEVELED OFF!

YES, SIR!

DIRECTOR! THAT GIRL!

FWOO

KLOMP

FWUD

THWAM

KAPOW

FWK

YOU
CAN
COME
OUT
NOW.

...SO THIS IS JUST FOR FUN.

I USUALLY WORK AT A JOB JUST LIKE ANYONE ELSE, THOUGH...

WHY DIDN'T YOU USE YOUR **POWER?**

HERO?

NO, YOU'RE **LYING.**

...I CAN'T USE IT ANY- MORE.

UM...

...THAT THEY MIGHT LET YOU OUT OF HERE.

YOU THOUGHT IF YOU SUPPRESSED YOUR **POWER**...

NO ONE IN HERE OR OUT THERE NEEDS ME.

IT DOESN'T MATTER ANY-MORE.

MAMA AND PAPA **SOLD** ME!

YOUR DEAR LITTLE SISTER.

NO, SOMEONE **DOES** NEED YOU.

PAT

YOU MUST PROTECT YOUR FAMILY.

THOSE WHO POSSESS GREAT POWER...

OKAY? LET ME GIVE YOU SOME ADVICE.

"...MUST NEVER EXPECT SOMEONE TO SAVE THEM."

SO HANG IN THERE!

WE'RE ALL COMING TO SAVE YOU!

BIG SISTER!

CAN YOU HEAR ME?!

IT WOULD'VE BEEN EASIER FOR ME TO GET A SAMPLE IF SHE HAD BEEN OFF THE MARK A BIT.

TORNADO IS SUCH A BEAST!

BUT IT'S ALL DAMAGED ON A CELLULAR LEVEL!

IT DUG INTO THE EARTH LIKE ROOTS, HUH?

ARE THESE...

...THE REMAINS OF THE MONSTER KING?

HWUP

DEMON CYBORG!

HWOOMP

URGH!

EXCEL-LENT!

KLANK

GWOOSH

PUNCH 143: INTO THE ABYSS

HAH!

BOOSH

GAME OVER!

?!

BOOM

UH... YOU'RE WELCOME.

BUT I DIDN'T DO ANYTHING TO THE TANK TOP...

THANKS, MISS BLIZZARD!

MY TANK TOP IS SUDDENLY PROVIDING INCREASED AGILITY! I DIDN'T KNOW YOU HAD THAT POWER!

WOOOOOO

DEMON CYBORG...

KSHNK

I WANT TO COMBINE WITH YOU AND INTEGRATE OUR POWER CORES FOR MAXIMUM OUTPUT.

I'M RUNNING LOW ON ENERGY.

...I REQUEST YOUR ASSISTANCE.

...ARE YOU WITH ME?

IT MAY NOT WORK, BUT...

VREEE-EEET

CAUTION

⚠ POWER CORE NEAR DEPLETION

THEN HERE GOES!

YES, I AM WITH YOU.

VMM
M

HA! YOU'LL HAVE TO DO BETTER THAN HURL DEBRIS!

HUH?!

DRAGON
KING!

DRIVE KNIGHT, MY CORE COULD EXPLODE AT ANY MOMENT!

AT MY SIGNAL, SEPARATE IMMEDIATELY! UNDERSTOOD?

...PIECES OF JUNK!

YOU...

UMPH!

NOW'S YOUR CHANCE!

SHE STOPPED MOVING!

VICTORY IS **OURS.**

DARK
☆
ANGEL
☆
RUSH!

V
I
B
R
A
T
I
O
N
☆

!!

WHIRLING WIND!

FLOWING WATER!

KOOM

THEY DID IT!

HUH?

NO, NOT YET.

WOOO

PMM MM MM

BIG SIS?

GOOD! JUST A LITTLE MORE!

OH, YOU MEAN THIS?

IF ONLY IT COULD BE MOVED...

NO, THERE'S SOMETHING IMMENSELY HEAVY THERE.

CAN'T YOU GET **YOURSELF** OUT NOW?

WHAT **IS** THIS?

WHEW!

CRUNK

YES, THANKS!

BETTER NOW?

TOSS

SHOULD I **PULL** YOU?

W-WHAT IS THIS THING?

UGH!!

YIKES!!

NO, STAY BACK!

YOU MIGHT BREAK SOME-THING!

KTHUNK

I'M IN A DELICATE SITUATION HERE!

TCH!

MORE INTENSE RUMBLING ...

RMMM

WAH!

KRUMBL

KRUMBL

FLASH-KILL...

RRRRRRM

Flash-kill

WELL, BOULDERS AREN'T GONNA BREAK MY **ARM**.

USE YOUR HEAD.

THAT'S WHAT YOU WERE WORRIED ABOUT BREAKING ?!

THAT MUST BE TOR- NADO!

I SEE A GREEN LIGHT!

A LANCE OF LIGHT ...

!!

SHZZ

SO LONG!

NO.

I SHOULD HAVE JUST BLASTED THE WALL APART IF IT WAS GOING TO BREAK ANYWAY.

ARE YOU INSULTING MY SWORD?

FLASH-KILL SURE DIDN'T COME **OUT** IN A FLASH!

SNEAK

HM?

...

THIS'S MY CHANCE TO SLIP AWAY!

GWUP

WOOOO

OOOOO

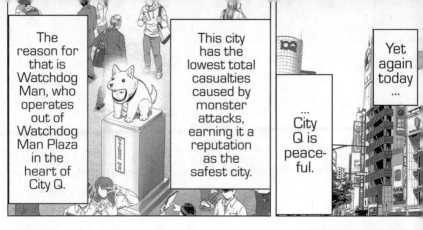

The reason for that is Watchdog Man, who operates out of Watchdog Man Plaza in the heart of City Q.

This city has the lowest total casualties caused by monster attacks, earning it a reputation as the safest city.

...City Q is peaceful.

Yet again today...

I'M SLEEPY.

YAWN

BONUS MANGA: SENSE OF SMELL

Whether attacks come by air...

...his sharp sense of smell immediately detects the monsters. He zips over at superspeed estimated at 250 kilometers per hour and dispatches the ne'er-do-wells within minutes.

?!

...or from underground...

He has even defeated monsters dozens of kilometers away before the local police could react.

That day, attacks came from multiple monsters estimated to be threat level Demon.

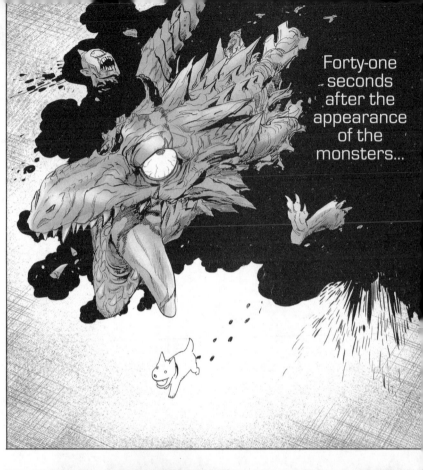

Forty-one seconds after the appearance of the monsters...

WATCHDOG MAN KILLED THEM ALL...

...BEFORE WE COULD SOUND THE ALARM!

NOW WE CAN'T ASSIGN A THREAT LEVEL.

FORGET BACKUP. CALL IN *CLEAN-UP.*

Yet again today, City Q is peaceful thanks to Watchdog Man.

...his full power.

And still no one knows...

28 Into the Abyss (End)

ONE-PUNCH MAN
VOLUME 28
SHONEN JUMP EDITION

STORY BY | ONE
ART BY | YUSUKE MURATA

TRANSLATION | JOHN WERRY
TOUCH-UP ART AND LETTERING | JAMES GAUBATZ
DESIGN | PAUL PADURARIU
EDITOR | JOHN BAE

ONE-PUNCH MAN © 2012 by ONE, Yusuke Murata
All rights reserved.
First published in Japan in 2012 by SHUEISHA Inc., Tokyo
English translation rights arranged by SHUEISHA Inc.

The stories, characters, and incidents mentioned in this
publication are entirely fictional.

Printed in the U.S.A.

Published by VIZ Media, LLC
P.O. Box 77010
San Francisco, CA 94107

10 9 8 7 6 5 4 3 2 1
First printing, May 2024

VIZ MEDIA
viz.com

SHONEN JUMP